The Grand Annual

by Brian Trueman

Book version by Nicholas Jones

Illustrations from the Cosgrove Hall production
Directed by Jackie Cockle

Thames Methuen

First published in Great Britain 1984
by Methuen Children's Books Ltd
11 New Fetter Lane, London EC4P 4EE
in association with Thames Television International Ltd
149 Tottenham Court Road, London W1P 9LL

Original storyline by Rosemary Anne Sisson

Printed in Great Britain

ISBN 0 423 01150 2

The unabridged edition of *The Wind in the Willows*
by Kenneth Grahame is available with full colour illustrations
from the award-winning Cosgrove Hall production.

The Cosgrove Hall film of the original book
by Kenneth Grahame is available on Thames Video

The Grand Annual Show

It was summer. The first freshness of the season, of green grass and dew-laden mornings, was over. Harvest-time was coming once more. The excitement of gathering in the fruits, of making sure for the winter, would reach everyone soon. But today it was only the dishes that Mole had gathered – after breakfast in the neat, hidden cosiness of Mole End. He felt that the effort might have earned him a sit-down and a cup of tea, when . . . clatter, slither, plop. A letter! Letters didn't come often to Mole End. Who could it be from? Not Badger, thought Mole. He was sociable enough once you got to know him – but he hardly ever *wrote* to anyone. And it couldn't be Toad – the paper wasn't *half* fancy enough. Mole savoured the uncertainty a moment more . . . then opened it . . . and read.

'O my, O my!' he exclaimed. 'How wonderful to win . . .! But then, of course, I never would . . .'

A letter arrived at Toad Hall, too, and it woke Toad. He sat up in bed.

'Post!' he announced to himself cheerfully.

'Letters from admirers! An invitation from the Palace . . .!' Having overcome the indignity, as he saw it, of having to fetch his own post, Toad clambered back into his ancestral four-poster, opened the envelope, and read the letter with almost as much delight as if it *had* been from the Palace . . .

Badger, on the other hand, had been out for a walk, bright and early as usual. When he returned, he found one of the young rabbits standing by his front door, examining a letter. The Rabbit didn't see Badger until the last moment, and he started guiltily:

'O! Er . . . 'morning, Mr Badger! Been out for your morning stroll, Sir?'

'I have,' said Badger, heavily.

'You . . . er . . . missed the postman, Sir!'

'Hmmm! But you, I see, did not! Off home with you!'

'Er . . . yes, Mr Badger,' muttered the thankful Rabbit, handing over the letter and scampering off.

'Hmph!' remarked Badger to himself. Better see what it says, I suppose.'

Now, as you may have guessed, all these letters were the same, and Ratty too was about to get one. When he heard the rattle of his letter box, he put aside the copy of the *Tatler* he was reading, and eagerly opened the envelope.

'Dear Field, River and Wild Wood Folk,' he read. 'This year, as usual, we are going to hold our Grand Annual Show' – 'O, splendid' – 'but with the additional attraction of a special Silver Cup, generously donated by Mrs M. F. H. Carrington-Moss, J.P., which will be awarded for the Best-of-Show in any class.'

'I say! What fun!' Ratty exclaimed to himself. He'd have time to bake one of his special walnut cakes! He thought a moment more: 'I wonder if the others have had an invitation too?'

There were several jars of blackcurrant jelly on the table in Mole's kitchen, and he was just standing back with a little sigh of satisfaction when he noticed that the handle of the spoon was still sticky.

He tried to lick the jelly off. 'O, bother!' Somehow, some of it had contrived to get on his glasses. He put the spoon down on the table – and, just too late, realised he'd put it on the recipe. 'O, now look what I've done!'

He took off his glasses to polish them on the edge of his apron, but the jelly was *so* sticky that it just smeared.

'O! Bother blackcurrant jelly! And bother the Silver Cup!'

And just at this tiresome moment, there was a knock at the door.

'O, blow! Come in!' said Mole, a little flustered.

It was Rat. 'I say, Mole, old chap, what are you up to?'

'O, Ratty! Why did I ever think I could . . . ?' Mole broke off, near to tears of frustration.

'Could what, old fellow?'

'Could make blackcurrant jelly, could enter it for Best-of-Show, could win the Cup!'

'Now, now, old chap! It *smells* glorious! It looks splendid!' Rat wiped his finger along the spoon handle, which was still sitting provocatively on the table, and tried a little. 'Mmmm! And it *tastes* wonderful!'

'Does it?' Mole ventured.

'It tastes like . . . like summer days, and autumn hedgerows, and winter tea-cakes . . . all rolled into one!' Rat enthused.

'Goodness, Ratty!' said a disbelieving but delighted Mole. 'Do you really think so?'

'I *do* really think so,' replied Rat. 'Shouldn't think my walnut cake will stand a chance.'

'Your walnut cake?' Mole was intrigued. 'You don't mean you're going in for Best-of-Show too?'

Rat, like the modest fellow he was, hadn't forceseen Mole's interest in his own entry, and was somewhat embarrassed at the prospect of admitting his earlier enthusiasm for the competition. So he replied, a little self-deprecatingly:

'Only for the fun of it. I don't much care about

winning the Best-of-Show Silver Cup – but, yes!'

Mole could sense his friend's discomfort:

'O, *I* don't *care* about it. I just thought I ought to join in.'

'Exactly,' agreed Rat, appreciating Mole's sensitivity. 'Er . . . you don't have any *walnuts*, I suppose!'

'O dear! I never keep them, Ratty. They disagree with me. But Badger does! He gathers them in the Wild Wood. He told me so.'

'Well, good old Badger! Might pop along and pay him a visit.'

Mole needed only a little encouragement to abandon his work. He'd had enough of kitchens, . . . and pans . . . and jam!

Rat and Mole found Badger in his kitchen – stabbing walnuts with a needle! Rat had timed his visit perfectly. He enquired if Badger had any to spare, and Badger replied, stabbing as he did so,

'Take as many' – stab – 'walnuts as you' – stab – 'need, my dear fellow! You can see I've' –

stab – 'plenty.' As he said 'plenty', Badger's concentration lapsed a little, and the next stab caught his thumb. Mole was naturally at first

concerned that the Badger had hurt himself, but the injury was clearly not serious, and Mole began to wonder about Badger's earnest determination.

'Dear, dear!' he voiced. 'Er . . . Badger . . . not that it's any of my business – but *why* are you stabbing those walnuts?'

'Going to pickle 'em, Mole, my boy!'
He paused, then added nonchalently, 'Besides, I might just enter a jar of 'em in the Annual Show. *If* I enter, it will merely be to support a local event!'

'Ah, yes! Of course!' said the Rat, suspecting that even Badger might be pleased if he won. But Badger dispelled such unjust questioning of his motives by adding, darkly, 'And so as to keep an eye on the others, who might see the Annual Show as an opportunity for showing off, like . . .'

'Toad!' Rat and Mole joined in. Rat could see that Badger had been his usual perceptive self and so they set off to pay a 'social call' on Toad Hall.

* * *

Toad was preparing his entry for the Show with his usual skill, patience, application, and modesty. On the table in the Great Hall, he was putting into practice his vision, a culmination of his extensive reading of *Great Wines of the World* and his exhaustive knowledge of chemistry imparted by years – well, days, anyway – of dedicated experimentation with his 'Chemistry Set No. 3'. All his equipment, both intellectual

and practical, would now come to fruition in a prizewinning vintage. Toad had no *audience,* but why should that prevent a recital of his skills?

'O chemistry! O *Toad*!
You clever, clever Toad!
You Isaac Newton of a Toad!
This is the way to make wine!
Côtes de Beaune? Pooh!
Mouton Cadet. Hoo!
The world will hear a new name, a great name: *Vin Spectaculaire de Château Toad*!'

And he sang a new verse of his song:

> As the Bishop sipped the nectar,
> His cheeks with pleasure glowed,
> 'Who makes this wond'rous wine,' he asked –
> They answered, 'Mr Toad!'
> De dumm, de dumm, de doo-doo . . .

'Ha, ha, ha! Bubble away, my miracle! Soon the world will be knocking at my door!'

Just as Toad said 'Door', there was a loud knock, for Badger, Ratty and Mole had arrived.

'Good heavens! *Already*!' said the astonished though delighted Toad. 'Ah, well! Genius will out!'

He went to welcome his visitors, musing upon who might have reacted so quickly. 'O, it's you!' he said when he saw them, scarcely concealing his disappointment.

'It is, Toad!' said Badger heavily. 'Who were you expecting?'

'Well, I thought . . . that is, I was expecting . . . well – come in, come in! Is it about the Silver Cup?'

'Well, yes, Toad! Matter of fact, it is!' Rat had to agree.

'Heavens, Toad!' Mole exclaimed, 'how *did* you know?'

'Inevitable, my dear fellow,' said Toad, airily indicating the wine-making equipment. 'All that . . . chemistry . . . the wonders of science . . . my *genius*! It was bound to get about. I've, er . . . saved a place for it on the mantlepiece.'

'Saved a place . . .' began Rat, incredulous.

'*One* moment, Toad!' Badger interrupted, with the verbal counterpart of a hand on Toad's shoulder. 'Am I to understand that you believe that you have as good as won the Best-of-Show award?'

'Well, yes, of course!' Toad said, confident as ever, adding in an aside to Rat, 'I do so hate false modesty, don't you?'

Badger continued doggedly. 'And for *what* have you as good as won it, Toad?'

'Hmmm? O, for my wine! For my home-brewed elderflower wine!'

Each listening animal took in this astonishing conceit – astonishing even by Toad's standards – and each reacted in his characteristic way: 'O, Toad!' said Mole, disapprovingly. Ratty had a slight edge to his voice as he said, 'O, really, Toad!' Badger adopted his most severe and gruff tone, and said: 'Toad! You are a wretched, conceited, self-deceiving animal!' But such admonishment was lost on Toad, who remained utterly sure of his skills:

'Not at all, my dear Badger! My wine will simply be the best in the world! It is the work of genius, it is!'

'It is altogether too much!' Badger interposed. 'Come on Rat! Let us leave this miserable animal to drown in his own conceit!'

Badger led the way, and Toad was left alone to remark to himself, 'Well, really! Tut! Ha! Jealousy does terrible things to a chap. Envy of my chemical genius . . .'

As he spoke, though, the bubbling noises coming from the Hall changed from a friendly burble to an angry, ominous rattling. 'I say! I wonder why it's making that funny noise? Perhaps I ought to . . .' Toad turned towards the Hall but – perhaps fortunately *before* he could reach the apparatus – there was a fearful explosion. When at last the smoke cleared, Toad was rather less dapper than his usual self, and the apparatus was little more than shimmering fragments of glass.

Such was Toad's temperament that disasters like this were instantly expressed in a torrent of self-pity:

'O, horror, O, despair! Dreams . . . shattered!
Ambitions . . . cast down!
Suit . . . absolutely ruined!
No more chemistry! No *Château Toad Hall*!
No Silver Cup!'

But even as he bewailed his misfortune, a sly look came over his face, and with, if the truth be told, a less-than-honourable thought in his mind, he set off for the cellar.

1st

On the day of the Show, the four friends were well satisfied. Each won his class. Even the Weasels had their success, and whilst some might not rejoice that it was so, one had to admit that their pumpkin was a most handsome fruit. Mole, in his generous way, remarked so to Badger: 'I say, haven't they done well?'

Then at last the moment came for the Best-of-Show. Mrs Carrington-Moss took the floor: 'The judges were quite unanimous in agreeing with me that, without doubt, the Best-of-Show Award of the Special Silver Cup goes to the Weasels' Wild Wood Allotment Society – for their magnificent pumpkin. So without more ado, and before I present the Cup, let me decorate the winning entry in the appropriate way.'

And she leaned forward to pin the rosette on the pumpkin. The result was extraordinary, for there was consternation among the Weasels – scarcely the reaction one would expect from proud prizewinners:

''Ere, lady! Knock it off!'

'No, no! Don't stick the . . .'

But she did – and there was a loud hissing as the pumpkin shrank and crumpled. It was a painted blown-up bladder! There was a gasp from the crowd, and Mrs Carrington-Moss stiffened.

'I see!' she admonished. 'Entering a pumpkin with intent to defraud! We'll see about that later . . .'

Even the Weasels were shamefaced at their unmasking.

'I wonder if – er . . . our bikes is all right?' said one.

'Eh?' replied his neighbour. 'We never came on no . . . Ah!' And they fled from the disapproving stare of the crowd.

'Well, in that case,' Mrs Carrington-Moss continued, 'I . . . er . . . *we* shall award the Best-of-Show to the Elderflower Wine entered by Mr Toad.'

Toad accepted this as only his rightful due: 'Hurray! Quite right! Genius will out! Well done, old girl!'

'O, not Toad!' exclaimed the Rat. 'He'll be insufferable!'

'*Will* be? Hugh!' Badger retorted.

Toad, indeed, was glorying in his success.

'Have a glass of wine, Mrs . . . er . . . Thingy! I give you a toast . . .' Toad held his bottle aloft. But he did not notice that the label had slipped, unstuck by its time in the wet ice-bucket. And beneath the label could be read another, less home-made one: '*Niederhauser Herrmanshole Spätlese*' it read. Mrs Carrington-Moss caught sight of it, and finished his toast for him, although not in quite the tone he had expected: 'Toad!'

'Yes?'

'I have that wine in my cellar!'

'Well, you needn't think I pinched it! *This* wine is from *my* cellar! And I . . .' He became aware that the approving chatter from the crowds around had changed to a *dis*approving mutter, and his voice tailed away.

'O . . . Toad!' said Ratty, Mole and Badger together, half sad at their friend's folly, half angry at his blatant conceit.

For once, Toad agreed with the Weasels as to the best course of action. 'I wonder if those poor fellows have found their bicycle?' he remarked, sidling away from the prize-giving.

In the silence which followed, voices were heard from outside the tent. It was the Fieldmice. 'Hang on! O, wait! Wait for us!' And they tottered in, struggling with a huge marrow.

'Sorry we're late! We had to *carry* it all the way after the wheelbarrow collapsed! Have we missed the judging?'

'On the contrary!' Mrs Carrington-Moss replied, admiringly. 'You're just in time to receive the award for Best-of-Show!'

This was a very popular choice. The crowds cheered, and Rat remarked:

'Well done, young 'uns! Put us *all* in our places!'

'And a good thing too!' added Badger. 'Now I think we had better follow Toad home. There are a few things I have to say to that unfortunate animal!'

They found a contrite Toad sobbing in Toad Hall:

'I can't think what came over me!'

'Just what always comes over you, Toad.' said Rat.

'Yes . . .' Badger thrust in quickly, 'greed, conceit, stupidity, lack of consideration.'

'O, I say! Steady on, Badger!' Toad complained.

But Badger continued: 'I should never have let you take part in a competition. It brings out the worst in all of us.'

'O, you're so right, my dear wise old Badger!

Never again shall I flaunt my skills as a wine-maker!'

'O, Toady!' Mole cried, admiring such determination from his friend.

Even Rat had to show his approval: 'Yes, well . . . er . . . good chap, Toad!' But he spoke too soon, for Toad added, irrepressibly:

'But come and have a look at my cauliflower!'

'Cauliflower!' 'O, Toad!'

'It's a miracle of science! Wait 'til next year – I'll give 'em pumpkins! I'll give 'em vegetable marrows . . .'

Ratty, Badger and Mole could only look at one another, aghast.